UNIVERSAL PICTURES STAGE PRODUCTIONS WORKING TITLE FILMS OLD VIC PRODUCTIONS
in association with **WEINSTEIN LIVE ENTERTAINMENT** present

Based on the Universal Pictures/Studio Canal Film

HAYDN GWYNNE   **GREGORY JBARA**
CAROLE SHELLEY   **SANTINO FONTANA**

And Introducing
DAVID ALVAREZ   TRENT KOWALIK   KIRIL KULISH

With

DAVID BOLOGNA • FRANK DOLCE • STEPHEN HANNA • JOEL HATCH • LEAH HOCKING • THOMMIE RETTER • ERIN WHYLAND
JULIETTE ALLEN ANGELO • TOMMY BATCHELOR • KEVIN BERNARD • GRADY McLEOD BOWMAN • HEATHER ANN BURNS • MARIA CONNELLY
SAMANTHA CZULADA • KYLE DesCHAMPS • EBONI EDWARDS • BRIANNA FRAGOMENI • GREG GRAHAM • ERIC GUNHUS • MEG GUZULESCU
IZZY HANSON-JOHNSTON • KEEAN JOHNSON • DONNIE KEHR • CARA KJELLMAN • KARA KLEIN • DAVID KOCH • JEFF KREADY • AARON KABURICK
STEPHANIE KURTZUBA • DAVID LARSEN • CAROLINE LONDON • MERLE LOUISE • MARINA MICALIZZI • MITCHELL MICHALISZYN
MATTHEW MINDLER • DARRELL GRAND MOULTRIE • TESSA NETTING • DANIEL ORESKES • JAYNE PATERSON • LIZ PEARCE
CORRIEANNE STEIN • JAMIE TORCELLINI • GRANT TURNER • CASEY WHYLAND

Press Representative	General Management	Advertising
BARLOW • HARTMAN	**NINA LANNAN ASSOCIATES/DEVIN KEUDELL**	**SPOTCO**

Production Stage Manager	Music Contractor	Production Supervisors
BONNIE L. BECKER	**MICHAEL KELLER**	**ARTHUR SICCARDI PATRICK SULLIVAN**

Adult Casting Director	Children's Casting Director	Resident Director
TARA RUBIN CASTING	**NORA BRENNAN**	**BT McNICHOLL**

Associate Set Designer	Associate Costume Designer	Associate Lighting Designer (Programmer)	Associate Sound Designer
PAUL ATKINSON	**CLAIRE MURPHY**	**VIC SMERDON**	**JOHN OWENS**

Associate Choreographer	Assistant Choreographer	Hair, Wig and Make-Up Designer
KATHRYN DUNN	**NIKKI BELSHER**	**CAMPBELL YOUNG**

Musical Supervision and Orchestrations by	Music Director
MARTIN KOCH	**DAVID CHASE**

Costume Design by	Lighting Design by	Sound Design by
NICKY GILLIBRAND	**RICK FISHER**	**PAUL ARDITTI**

Executive Producers
DAVID FURNISH   ANGELA MORRISON

Produced by
TIM BEVAN   ERIC FELLNER   JON FINN   SALLY GREENE

Associate Director	Set Design by	Choreography by
JULIAN WEBBER	**IAN MacNEIL**	**PETER DARLING**

Directed by	Book and Lyrics by	Music by
STEPHEN DALDRY	**LEE HALL**	**ELTON JOHN**

PRESENTED BY FIDELITY INVESTMENTS

Cover art courtesy of Serino Coyne

978-1-4234-6480-8

7777 W. BLUEMOUND RD. P.O. BOX 13819 MILWAUKEE, WI 53213

Visit Hal Leonard Online at
www.halleonard.com

CONTENTS

THE STARS LOOK DOWN

Music by ELTON JOHN
Lyrics by LEE HALL

SHINE

Music by ELTON JOHN
Lyrics by LEE HALL

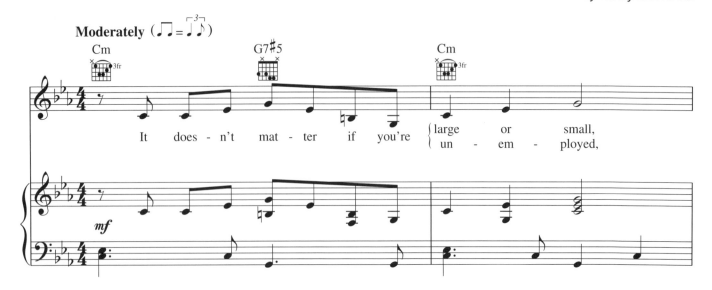

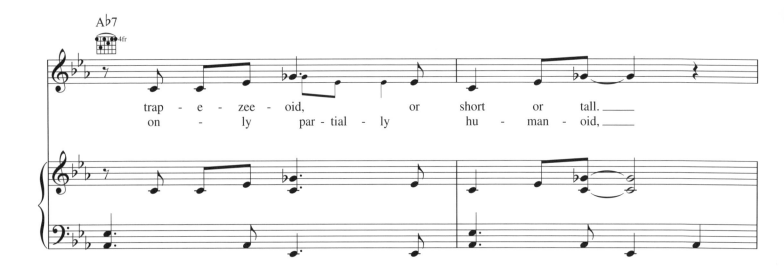

Show them what life is all a - bout! ___
Show them what class is

Give 'em the old ___ raz - zle - daz - zle, and

To Coda ⊕

shine! *(Spoken:)* Go on, join in! I dare you!

shine! _____

Slower, expressively (♩♩ = ♩♩)

You might be feel - ing lous - y, _____

-ver it; ____ it's all part of the gig!

D.S. al Coda

N.C.

Disco style (♩♩ = ♩♩)

CODA

E♭   Fm/B♭   E♭   G/D

shine! _____

Cm   G7♯5   Cm

It does - n't mat - ter if you're short or squat, ___

A♭7

cer - e - bral - ly chal - lenged, com - plete - ly shot; ___

GRANDMA'S SONG

Music by ELTON JOHN
Lyrics by LEE HALL

SOLIDARITY

Music by ELTON JOHN
Lyrics by LEE HALL

POLICE:
Oi, Geor - die, wan - na see some-thing you
Keep it up 'til Christ - mas, lads, __ it

nev - er seen __ be - fore? __ And that's just off the o - ver-time.
means a lot __ to us. __ We'll send our kids to pri - vate school

Wan - na see __ some more? __ You think you're smart, __ you cock - ney shite! You
on a pri - vate bus. __ We've got a lot __ to thank you for, __

(1.) MINERS:
(2.) (POLICE):

32

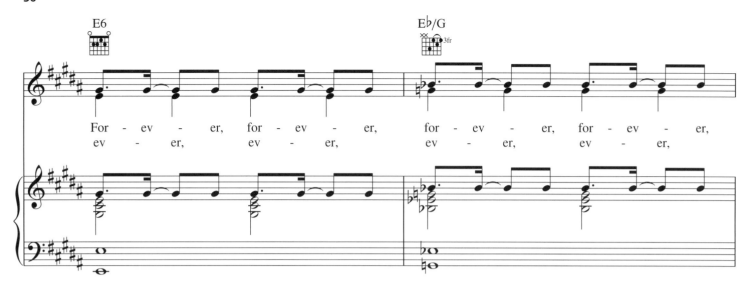

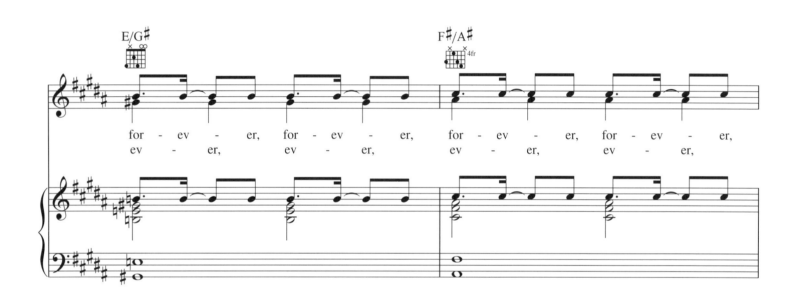

ev-er and ev-er, and ev-er and ev-er, and ev-er and ev-er, and ev-er and ev'r. For-

for - ev - er, for - ev - er, for - ev - er, for - ev'r. _

ev - er, ev - er, ev - er, ev - er.

ev - er and ev - er and ev -

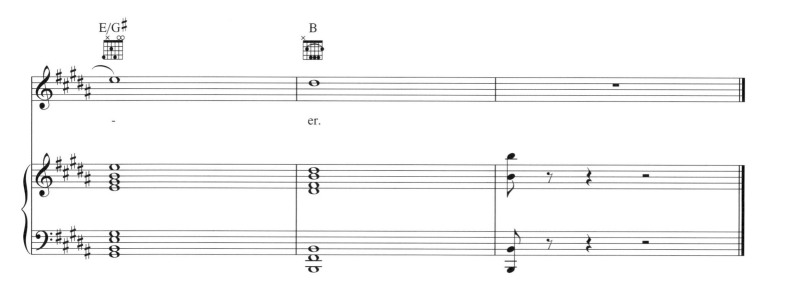

- er.

EXPRESSING YOURSELF

Music by ELTON JOHN
Lyrics by LEE HALL

THE LETTER

Music by ELTON JOHN
Lyrics by LEE HALL

BORN TO BOOGIE

Music by ELTON JOHN
Lyrics by LEE HALL

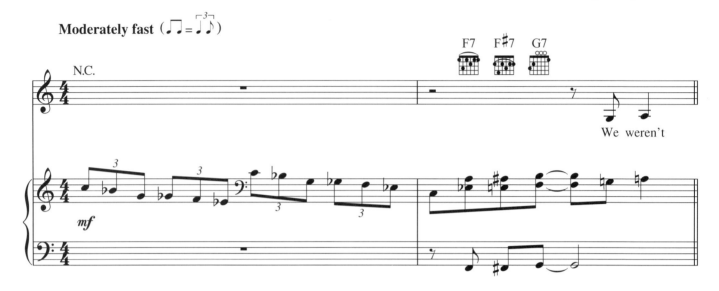

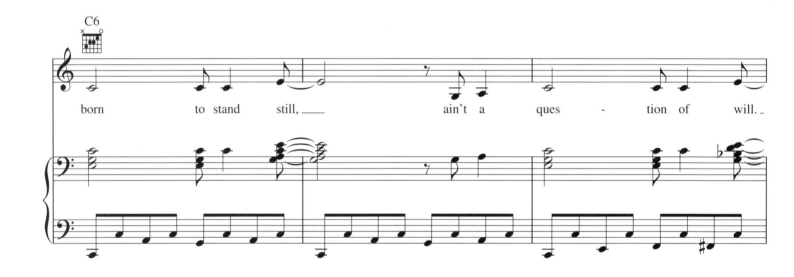

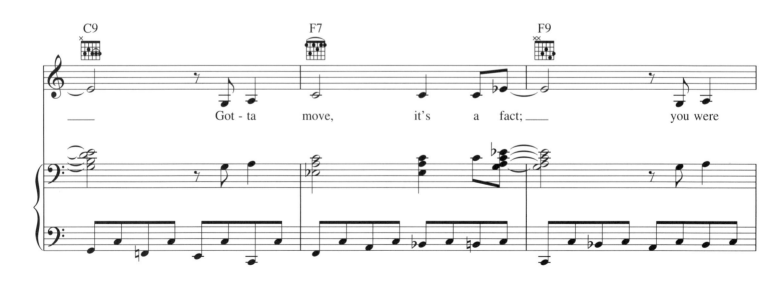

MERRY CHRISTMAS MAGGIE THATCHER

Music by ELTON JOHN
Lyrics by LEE HALL

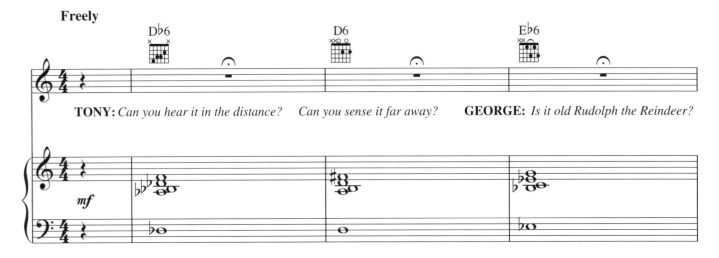

Freely

TONY: *Can you hear it in the distance? Can you sense it far away?* GEORGE: *Is it old Rudolph the Reindeer?*

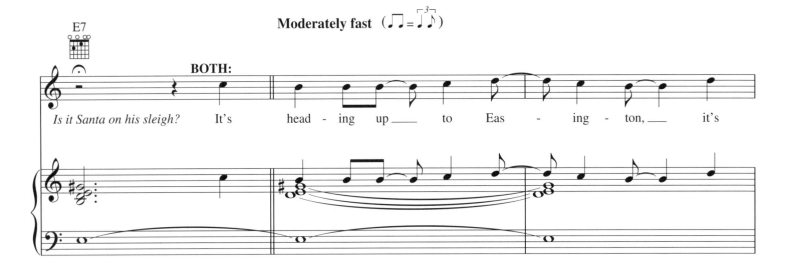

Is it Santa on his sleigh? BOTH: It's head-ing up___ to Eas-ing-ton,___ it's

Moderately fast

com-ing down___ the Tyne.___ ALL: Oh, it's blood-y Mag-gie Thatch-

accel.

C

to raid your stock - ings, and to steal ____

their fas - cist boot - boys, and they've brought ____

Am

your Christ - mas pud', ____ but don't ____

the boys in blue, ____ and the whole ____

F

be too down - heart - ed; it's all ____

Trades Un - ion Con - gress will be at ____

G

for your ____ own good. ____ The

the par - ty too. ____ And they'll all ____

DEEP INTO THE GROUND

Music by ELTON JOHN
Lyrics by LEE HALL

HE COULD BE A STAR

Music by ELTON JOHN
Lyrics by LEE HALL

Moderately

DAD:
I could-n't take it an-y-more, son, it was tear-ing me a-part. We're
not a-bout the kid. It's

lost, we're fin-ished, man, __ we're through. I need to give
all of us, it's ev-'ry-bod __ y's chance. It's

ELECTRICITY

Music by ELTON JOHN
Lyrics by LEE HALL

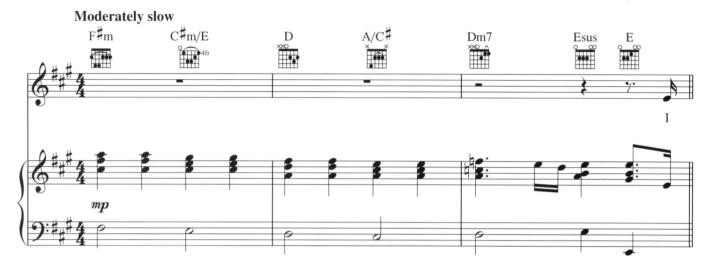

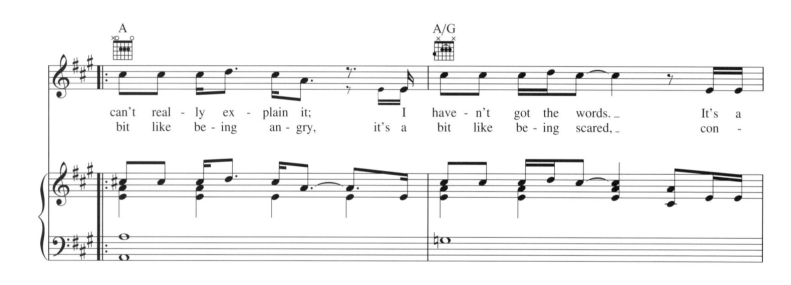

can't real-ly ex-plain it; I have-n't got the words._ It's a
bit like be-ing an-gry, it's a bit like be-ing scared,_ con -

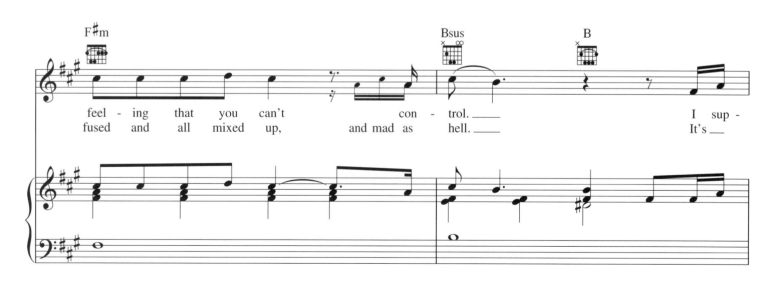

feel-ing that you can't con-trol. _____ I sup-
fused and all mixed up, and mad as hell. _____ It's ___

ONCE WE WERE KINGS

Music by ELTON JOHN
Lyrics by LEE HALL